HOWZAT!

Written by Paul Mason
Illustrated by Nicolas Hitori De

Published by Pearson Education Limited, Edinburgh Gate, Harlow, Essex, CM20 2JE.

www.pearsonschools.co.uk

Text © Pearson Education Limited 2013
Original illustrations © Nicolas Hitori De 2013
Illustrated by Nicolas Hitori De

The right of Paul Mason to be identified as author of this work has been asserted by him in accordance with the Copyright, Designs and Patents Act 1988.

First published 2013

17 16 15 14 13
10 9 8 7 6 5 4 3 2 1

British Library Cataloguing in Publication Data
A catalogue record for this book is available from the British Library

ISBN 978 0 435 14377 0

Copyright notice
All rights reserved. No part of this publication may be reproduced in any form or by any means (including photocopying or storing it in any medium by electronic means and whether or not transiently or incidentally to some other use of this publication) without the written permission of the copyright owner, except in accordance with the provisions of the Copyright, Designs and Patents Act 1988 or under the terms of a licence issued by the Copyright Licensing Agency, Saffron House, 6–10 Kirby Street, London EC1N 8TS (www.cla.co.uk). Applications for the copyright owner's written permission should be addressed to the publisher.

Printed and bound in Dubai by Oriental Press.

Acknowledgements
We would like to thank Bangor Central Integrated Primary School, Northern Ireland; Bishop Henderson Church of England Primary School, Somerset; Bletchingdon Parochial Church of England Primary School, Oxfordshire; Brookside Community Primary School, Somerset; Bude Park Primary School, Hull; Carisbrooke Church of England Primary School, Isle of Wight; Cheddington Combined School, Buckinghamshire; Dair House Independent School, Buckinghamshire; Deal Parochial School, Kent; Glebe Infant School, Gloucestershire; Henley Green Primary School, Coventry; Lovelace Primary School, Surrey; Our Lady of Peace Junior School, Slough; Tackley Church of England Primary School, Oxfordshire; and Twyford Church of England School, Buckinghamshire for their invaluable help in the development and trialling of the Bug Club resources.

Every effort has been made to contact copyright holders of material reproduced in this book. Any omissions will be rectified in subsequent printings if notice is given to the publishers.

Contents

A New Innings   *5*

Kite Fight   *34*

A New Innings

CHAPTER 1

Jamie stared at the wicker basket resting on the grass, wary of what lay coiled inside. In front sat the charmer, legs tucked underneath his robes, a crisp, cotton turban on his head. The charmer reached for his flute, and as the warbling began, the music clinging to the air like treacle, Jamie shuffled back.

A long dark shape appeared from the gloom, as thick as Jamie's wrist, shiny skin flickering in the sunlight. A cobra. Up it rose, its neck fanned out, dark haunting circles like eyes stared from the back of its hood.

Jamie's mum leaned over. "You wouldn't get this back home in England, would you?" she whispered in his ear.

Jamie had to admit she was right; this was pretty cool. He was spellbound by the warm breeze, the syrupy flute music, the gently swaying cobra. Had he been more aware, Jamie might have spotted his pet rabbit hopping towards them, nose twitching.

In an instant, the cobra's dark, shiny eyes changed direction, head swivelling, hood puffing even larger. Then before anyone could blink, it shot out of the basket, a black blur striking out across the grass.

"Watch it!" Jamie shouted.

The cobra moved like the flick of a whip. The rabbit leaped for cover and the snake charmer launched himself to one side, arm outstretched, fingers clawing. The snake moved to strike — but then with a jerk it sprang back, its tail caught in the charmer's strong grip.

The charmer held the writhing serpent at arm's length. Reaching for his stick, he forced the cobra back into the basket and slammed down the lid. It was all over in a flash.

Jamie found the rabbit trembling under a shrub against the wall. He picked it up, the little rabbit's heart thumping under his hands. Jamie stormed past the snake charmer and into the house.

"It's okay, Jamie," he could hear his mum calling out after him. "It's okay."

Later she found Jamie in his room, sitting on his bed with the rabbit.

Jamie looked up, scowling. "It's not okay," were the first words out of his mouth. "Snakes. This weird city — Lahore. I don't like it here. None of it's okay." He shook his head.

The present was a cricket bat, a full-sized one, with a light wooden blade and an orange grip. It felt heavy, solid. Jamie twirled it between his hands, the toe of the bat resting on the floor.

"It's a good one," said Jamie's dad. "The England skipper himself wouldn't mind having one of those."

Jamie grinned. "Thanks Dad," he said, eyes wide.

"I thought maybe you might like to join in with some of the local lads," Jamie's dad suggested.

Jamie pictured the large open cricket ground, a short bike ride away. A cricket match was always on: the pitch set, the batsmen padded up, the bowlers charging in. They weren't just fun knock-arounds in a park though; they were hard fought games. Jamie hesitated. He wasn't so sure about joining in.

"Maybe," he said slowly.

"It's not all bad," his mum sighed. "It'll get better."

"Can't we just go back to England? I don't see why Dad had to take this job in Pakistan."

"We didn't have much choice," explained Jamie's mum and sat down beside him.

They were silent for a few moments, both thinking wistfully of the life they had left behind.

Some jangling Urdu pop music drifted in from the kitchen radio. Then came the screeching voice of Altab, the cook, as he broke into song. Jamie groaned.

"At least Altab's food is better than his singing," laughed Jamie's mum.

"True," Jamie smiled.

"Anyway, Dad will be home soon," said his mum. "I seem to remember him mentioning something about a present," she said with a teasing look in her eyes.

"Oh come on – you'll be great," said Jamie's dad. "You were in the school team weren't you?"

With a bat like this one, perhaps his dad was right. Jamie nodded, "I guess I could give it a go."

CHAPTER 2

The next morning, after he'd let his rabbit out of its hutch and before the sun had climbed too high, Jamie grabbed his bat and pads and pedalled off on his bike, shouting a quick goodbye to his mum.

He reached the edge of the large ground where the grass was brown and dry. A cricket match was already underway. Jamie found a tree on the boundary and swerved to a stop. He got out his gear but decided he'd just watch for a while. Some of the boys from the batting team looked over at Jamie and pointed.

As he watched, Jamie could see the ball was really zipping off the hard pitch. The bowler was good, that much Jamie could tell. Head and shoulders above the others. A fast ball, a clatter of stumps, and the batsman was out, slinking off the pitch.

Just then a boy from the batting team ran over towards Jamie. "*Assalamu alaykum*," he said, tilting his head as he spoke. Then hesitantly in English, "What is your name?"

"Jamie."

"My name is Ali," said the boy, shaking Jamie's hand. "Can you play?" he asked hopefully, nodding at the bat and pads.

"A little."

"Great!" said the boy with a smile. "My team is short. You will play, yes?"

Jamie hesitated. "Okay. When?"

"Now!" said Ali pointing to the pitch. "You're the last man!"

Jamie did up his pads as fast as he could and before he had time to think, he was jogging out to the middle, swinging his bat.

He took a quick look around the field and set himself up at the batting crease. He gave the pitch a few taps with his new bat and turned to face the bowler, who seemed to tower at the other end, a fierce look in his eye. Jamie's throat was tight, and if he could have walked off the pitch then and there, he would have. But it was too late for that now.

The bowler sprinted in towards the wicket, gathering speed as he ran. The ball flew out of the bowler's hand and hit the pitch, hard and fast – a bouncer, first ball!

It fizzed off the surface and climbed rapidly. Jamie closed his eyes; he just couldn't help it.

THUD! Jamie felt the ball smack high into his ribs, like a sharp jab from a boxer. Pain jolted through his body and he dropped his bat and fell, trying hard not to cry out. His bat hit the pitch and clattered into the stumps. Through blurred eyes, Jamie saw the umpire raise his finger.

Out! He'd lasted one ball.

The bowler stood there, hands on his hips, a big grin on his face. There was no apology, no checking to see if Jamie was all right, just an ugly smile. The boy shook his head, saying something in Urdu. Jamie caught the word "*Angraize*" – English.

Tears forced their way out of Jamie's eyes and down his cheek.

He quickly wiped them away with the back of his hand. He should never have come. He didn't belong in this place.

Ali ran over, glaring angrily at the bowler as he passed him.

"Sohail is a bully," he said gesturing over at the bowler. "Are you all right?"

"Yeah, I think so," said Jamie rubbing his chest. "I'm sorry I got out."

"No problem," said Ali. "The match was lost anyway. They are much better than us."

The two of them wandered off the field towards Jamie's bike. Jamie's head was pounding; he just wanted this day to end. "I'll think I'll head home now," he said.

"Where is your house?" asked Ali. He smiled when Jamie told him. "That is near my street! Come!"

Jamie glanced over at the others as they walked off. Sohail was still standing there, arms folded, still smirking. Somehow Jamie knew that their paths would cross again.

CHAPTER 3

The boys took the road that ran through the bazaar, a sprawling local market with dirt roads that were heaving with crowds and the call of hawkers. There were fruit sellers with great baskets of bright oranges piled high; vegetable stalls with pyramids of produce and bunches of herbs; butchers with huge wooden chopping boards and hunks of meat hanging from hooks. There were horse-drawn carts and men pushing bicycles heavy with goods.

Ali weaved his way through the confusion, Jamie following. At last they reached Jamie's street. "This is where I live," he said.

Ali broke into a smile again. "And my house is just round the corner. We are neighbours, yes?"

"Neighbours," Jamie agreed.

"Some more cricket?" suggested Ali.

Jamie rubbed the spot where the ball had hit him. "Okay," he said. "Why not?"

Ali led him to his house, opening up the tall, metal gate, and went through to the shaded garden at the back. Some stumps were set up at the end of the lawn.

"Cricket ..." said Ali, "... but first some *lassi*. Please sit." Ali gestured towards some chairs.

Ali disappeared into the house and came out a few minutes later with two tall glasses of what looked like milk. He handed one to Jamie who took a sip. It was wonderful

– cold, sweet yoghurt, smooth like a milkshake. He pressed the cool glass against his forehead.

"Always keep your eye on the ball. You should never close your eyes!" said Ali, once they had drained their glasses.

Jamie looked at his feet. "I know. It was a mistake."

Ali picked up the cricket ball lying on the grass and gripped it. "Watch the ball in the bowler's hands. Then follow the ball all the way." Jamie nodded. "Come on, let's practise."

Jamie picked up his new bat again, talking to it under his breath. Ali twirled the ball from hand to hand, and once Jamie was ready, he ran in.

The boys practised for the rest of the afternoon. Jamie faced ball after ball, his bat feeling ever more solid, his footwork confident, his hands relaxed.

"How did the cricket go?" Jamie's mum asked when he got home. "I was beginning to wonder where you'd got to."

"It started off ropey, but turned out all right in the end," said Jamie with a smile.

Later on, after dinner, Jamie and his mum were watching television when suddenly everything went black. The TV, the lights, Altab's radio, everything died.

"Blackout," Jamie's mum sighed. "I'll get the candles."

Another power cut, thought Jamie. They were always happening.

His mum came back, candlelight dancing on her face. "Come upstairs," she whispered, "up on the roof. I've got a surprise for you."

Jamie followed his mum up the concrete stairs. The roof of the house was flat, like many on the street, and Jamie could just make out the shape of a charpoy – one of the wood and rope beds they slept on.

"I asked Altab to move the spare one up earlier," his mum explained. "I thought you might like a treat as Dad is away again. We could stare up at the stars for a while; the blackout gives us the perfect excuse."

Jamie looked out across the city. Everything as far as he could see was totally black. In a power cut, it was as if Lahore

almost didn't exist, a phantom city. But it was the sky that was really amazing. Jamie had never seen so many stars. With no light coming from the city, the sky was lit up with clouds of tiny, flickering pinpricks. For the first time, Jamie understood why it was called the Milky Way.

"Pretty cool, eh?" said his mum, as they gazed up. She pulled a light shawl over her shoulders.

"Brilliant," Jamie agreed. Then he added, "You were right, Mum. Things are getting better."

CHAPTER 4

That weekend, Ali persuaded Jamie to come back to the cricket ground and play. He saw the look on Jamie's face. "You're ready. No problem," he said with a smile.

At the ground, looking over at the other team, Jamie still wasn't sure. Sohail was busy warming up, turning his arm over, a look of scorn fixed on his face. He caught Jamie's eye and smiled at him. Jamie looked away.

By the time it was Jamie's turn to bat, the match was already well and truly lost.

"It's not been good," Ali admitted as Jamie prepared to go out. "Only a few balls more. Might as well have fun. Now remember, keep your eye on the ball."

Jamie nodded and jogged out to the field. As Jamie passed the fielding team in their huddle, Sohail looked over and muttered something in Urdu. The rest of the boys laughed – cackling, cruel sniggers.

If Jamie's heart had been thumping the first time he faced Sohail, now it was thrashing inside his chest. He glanced around the field, swallowing hard.

Sohail tossed the ball from hand to hand, a fierce look in his eyes. Jamie clamped his jaw tight and watched as Sohail reached the end of his run, watched him as he leaped into the air, watched him bring his arm round in a blur.

Sohail's first ball was full-bowled right at Jamie's toes at real pace – a yorker. Jamie followed it all the way, and jabbed his bat down to try and keep it out. The ball thumped into his pads.

"Howzat!" A harsh shout, more like a roar, came from Sohail as he appealed to the umpire. The umpire shook his head. Not out. Sohail kicked at the ground in disgust. Jamie let out a long breath. Close call, but he'd survived the first one.

Next ball and Jamie thrust out his bat, a blocking, defensive shot. There was a knock, a solid knock, and the ball ran back to Sohail's feet. Jamie smiled; it was good to feel the bat controlling the ball.

This time, Sohail paused at the top of his run up and gestured at his fielders, getting them exactly where he wanted them. Then he broke into a jog. Faster and faster his legs flew – galloping into the crease. Sohail sprung into the air and, in one smooth action, brought the ball down fast.

Jamie tracked the ball as it left Sohail's hands. He knew he had to focus because it was all so quick. Sohail had really bent his back into this one. Jamie took a stride forward, jaw clenched, and swung his bat.

He watched the ball fall onto the blade. Watched it all the way. CRACK! He struck it off the middle. In a flash, the ball raced across the field towards the boundary. Four!

Sohail snarled. He wiped the sweat off his brow and waited impatiently for one of the fielders to throw the ball back to him. Now he worked one side of the red ball against his trousers, trying to give it a bit more shine so that it would swing awkwardly through the air.

Jamie could see he'd really got under Sohail's skin. Sohail was losing his cool.

Down Sohail charged again, legs pumping, the hard, leather ball in his grip. The ball hit the deck with a thump and shot up – another short ball, another bouncer. This time Jamie was expecting it. He swivelled smartly on his back foot, and CRACK, he hooked the ball, high into the air, a clattering shot.

Then everything seemed to slow down.

Jamie could hear "Caaatch," roaring across the field from Sohail. He could see the ball sailing towards the boundary, a fielder scrambling to get into position under it. He could see the umpire turning his head. But there was no way the fielder was going to get anywhere near it.

At that moment, Jamie thought about everything that had happened: the move to a country where things seemed so different, and where he felt so lost; the darting cobra; Sohail's cruel blow to the ribs. All of that fell away. As the ball flew over the boundary and disappeared into the distance, Jamie could only think about the bat in his hands, his new friend and how good things were.

The umpire raised both hands in the air and Jamie could hear Ali and the others cheering. Six!

His heart racing, Jamie marched up the pitch and stared straight into Sohail's eyes. "How's that?" he said with a grin.

Kite Fight

CHAPTER 1

The cannon stood firm in the afternoon haze, its mighty brass barrel pointing straight at the two boys, its giant wooden wheels towering over them. Jamie ran his hands along the length of the cannon. The metal was warm to the touch. It must have seen many battles in its day. Now it just rested quietly on its marble platform, watching over the heart of Lahore.

"I'm going to climb up," Ali announced. He stood on one of the wooden wheels and grabbed at the spokes.

"Are you sure?" Jamie asked. He didn't think you were allowed to climb the cannon, but Ali had soon pulled himself up and was sitting astride the giant barrel. Jamie glanced around. Traffic roared down the road on either side of them. Some pigeons strutted at the far end of the platform, but they were otherwise alone.

Jamie raised his foot onto one of the spokes and pushed himself up too. A moment later he was sitting opposite Ali, legs dangling over the sides, gazing out at the city from their perch.

Jamie looked towards the park, just past the roundabout. Above the trees, dancing on the afternoon breeze there were kites. At least a dozen of them were cutting through the air.

Ali followed Jamie's gaze. "Basant," he said. "They are practising kite flying."

"Basant?" Jamie was confused.

"Kite festival – biggest in whole of Pakistan." Ali smiled. "So many people fighting with kites, every roof is filled with people. The whole sky will be covered, like birds. You won't believe it, Jamie."

"Fighting with kites?" queried Jamie.

"You don't know this?"

Jamie shook his head. Ali's face lit up as he talked, mimicking holding a kite string, his eyes gazing up to the sky. "My kite is in the sky, flying strong. Then, there comes another, each trying to get the upper hand. Waiting, dancing, then a tangle, and …" he suddenly jerked on the imaginary line.

"*Bo kata!* You cut their string."

"Cut?"

"String is very sharp, when coated with glass powder," Ali grinned.

"Sounds cool," said Jamie.

Just then came a whistle, a sharp blast cutting through the grumbling of the traffic. A policeman picked his way through the procession of cars and motorbikes, whistle in his mouth, bamboo *lathi* in his hand. Ali's smiled faded.

"Off, off!" the policeman hissed crossly at the boys.

Jamie quickly swung his legs off the barrel and clambered down as the policeman reached them. The policeman wagged his finger at Jamie, "No!" he said sharply, then directed a stream of Urdu at Ali.

Ali looked at his feet. "*Theek hay*," he said to the policeman. "Okay, he says we must go now."

The policeman escorted the two of them off the platform and back over the road towards the museum. He gave them a final glare and then marched off, his *lathi* tucked under his arm.

Jamie let out a long sigh but Ali just shrugged. They waited on the grass outside the entrance of the museum until, at last, Jamie's mum came out.

"You boys really should have taken more of a look inside," she said.

"We've been looking at the cannon," Jamie explained.

"Ah, it's called Zam-Zammah – the lion's roar," said Jamie's mum. "It was made famous in a book called *Kim*. The book starts with the main character climbing on it."

Jamie and Ali exchanged glances.

"Let's find a taxi and head back, shall we?" said Jamie's mum.

When they got close to their neighbourhood, Ali turned to Jamie's mum. "If it is okay Mrs Clayton, can we stop at the bazaar? I want to show Jamie something."

Jamie's mum asked the driver to pull over. "Be back in time for dinner, Jamie," she smiled.

"Sure, Mum," said Jamie as they clambered out.

"What are you going to show me?" he asked Ali as they watched the black and yellow taxi drive off.

"Come," said Ali.

Ali ducked down one of the side streets and suddenly the boys found themselves surrounded by colour. Reds and oranges spread around them like flames. There were

lush greens and blazes of yellow. Kites: some like sharp-edged diamonds, others more like birds. Shop after shop of kites, the whole street was full of them.

Ali stopped in front of one of the stalls. "There!" he said, pointing. "That's the one. The one we will fly on Basant."

CHAPTER

The kite hanging on the wall was like nothing Jamie had seen before. It seemed like a giant bird of prey from a legend, turned into paper and bound by a thin, bamboo frame. From its sharp head to the sweep of its wide tail, it stood tall, half as tall as Jamie himself; rounded orange wings spread wide, the pointed tips bright blue. It was magnificent.

The kite seller lifted the kite down and dangled it in front of Ali, holding it by a string attached to the head. Jamie could see Ali's eyes widen as he ran his fingers over the glorious kite.

Then Ali examined the spools of brightly coloured string on offer. The kite seller unravelled a few of them to show Ali their quality.

Ali ran his finger slowly over the threads before choosing a spool of red. "This is good *dor*. Strong and sharp," he explained to Jamie. "Good for fighting."

"*Kitne paise?*" Ali asked. His face fell when the kite seller told him how much the kite and the string would cost.

Ali shook his head. "It is far too many rupees," he said. "I don't have that much."

"What if we went halves?" Jamie asked. He fished out his wallet where he still had most of his month's pocket money. "You can teach me how to fly it," he added.

Ali beamed. "Agreed!" He reached into his pocket and brought out a few carefully folded notes.

Ali and the kite seller haggled for a bit, and then Ali handed the shopkeeper a few more notes. Finally the shopkeeper tilted his head in agreement. Together with Jamie's money there was just enough.

"Ali!" a harsh voice called out. The boys turned and their hearts dropped. It was Sohail, their rival from the cricket pitch. A group of boys were following him down the street.

Sohail flicked his head back in a scornful greeting, his eyes full of contempt. *No surprise there,* thought Jamie. He remembered the first time he'd had to face up to Sohail in a cricket match. The bigger boy had greeted him with a harsh bouncer that had left him with a painful, purple bruise on his ribs.

Sohail and the others came up to Ali and stood closely around him in a circle, eyeing the kite. *"Bahutaccha,* very good," Sohail nodded.

He reached out and touched the edge of the frame. Ali flinched a little, though he tried to hide it.

"*Theek hai,* I won't hurt your kite," Sohail sniggered. He turned to his friends. "We want this kite in good order. For when we take it on Basant."

"We'll see," said Ali.

Sohail slapped Ali hard on the back. "Every year you try to beat me, Ali. Every year same story. *Angraize* here isn't going to help you." Jamie felt his face redden.

Sohail laughed again and gestured for his friends to follow him. "See you on Basant," he called back.

"This year I know we can beat him," said Ali, but the worried look in his eyes said otherwise.

CHAPTER 3

On the eve of Basant they chose Jamie's roof to stage their battles. It was a storey taller than Ali's house, and had a waist-high wall running around its edge which made it safe. Up here they were above the telephone and power lines. Perched above the neighbourhood they would have a good vantage point.

Jamie stared across the rooftops as dusk was falling over the city. On some of the flat roofs around them families and friends were already gathering. The beating of drums floated on the warm breeze along with the smell of charcoal fires and sizzling kebabs. The festival had begun, and he and Ali were ready to battle.

Ali finished tying the string to the kite, a plain white one. "The night before Basant, everyone is flying white kites – easy to see in the dark," he explained. They were saving the kite they had nicknamed *Shaheen*, the falcon, for the next day.

Ali handed the kite to Jamie telling him to hold it steady. Jamie backed up to the end of the roof. Ali reeled out the line and made it tight.

"Ready?" he called out and Jamie nodded, the kite straining in his outstretched arms. "Go!"

Jamie launched the fragile, paper structure up into the sky. Ali jerked the line to create tension, and let it out again as the greedy kite swallowed the wind, hungry for more. Soon the kite was soaring through the evening air, tissue paper rattling, joining the others as they darted like shadows across the dimly-lit sky.

"*Pecha!*" Ali shouted across the rooftops with a smile, the call to battle. "Now watch me pulling the line in, then letting it out," he said to Jamie. "You must do the same. We work together."

Jamie handled the spool of string, making sure Ali had enough to play out, but not too much to get tangled. Jamie laughed. He couldn't help himself. In the darkening sky, with the houses lit up, the white kites looked like giant moths dancing above the rooftops, circling the light.

Now from a house at the end of the street the battle cry was returned *"Pecha!"* A group of boys were jumping up and down, arms in the air. Jamie wasn't sure, but he thought it was Sohail's gang.

Ali nodded. "Sohail," he muttered, peering out at the rooftop.

The lights on the roof came on, and Jamie's mum came up with lemonade. "Some *nimbu pani* for my paper pilots," she teased.

Ali handed Jamie the line, showing him how to keep the line tight between his thumb and forefinger. *"Shukriya,"* he said politely to Jamie's mum, taking a glass.

"Pull, and the kite dives; let it loose and it will slow," he explained to Jamie.

"So, how's it going?" Jamie's mum asked, gazing up at their kite.

"We're about to fight," said Jamie jerking the line the way Ali had showed him. "Want to stay and watch?"

"Wouldn't miss it!" replied his mum, settling herself down on one of the chairs.

Ali took the string from Jamie. "Ready?" he chuckled. "Be quick on the line!"

Ali guided the kite, now just a pale phantom hovering in the distance, towards where they'd seen Sohail and the others.

"*Pecha!*" Ali shouted. Again came the reply through the darkness. It was time for the kites to tangle.

Jamie watched Ali's hands as he pulled the line, back and forth, the white moth dancing above them. Sohail's kite swooped down to join in the fray.

Almost immediately, Ali cried out, "No!" The lines were wrapped around each other, there was a tug, and their line went slack. They saw their kite drift off, lifeless and limp, ready to be captured by the children running on the pavements below.

A shout of "*Bo kata!*" roared out of the darkness. Success!

Ali helped Jamie reel their string back in, not saying a word, the beating of the drums now sounding like taunts.

"Wait till tomorrow," Ali muttered. "Then we'll see."

CHAPTER 4

By the time Jamie swung open the roof door the following morning, hundreds of kites already dotted the Lahore sky, like a flock of paper birds on the wing. Out across the city there were coloured specks as far as Jamie could see – and on each rode the chance of jubilation or despair. Already, cries of battle filled the neighbourhood.

Still reeling from the kite they had lost to Sohail the night before, Jamie and Ali unleashed *Shaheen* towards the blue sky. If Ali had lost any confidence at Sohail's hands, he didn't show it. Jamie noticed that he'd even put on his best *shalwar kameez* for the occasion.

Ali tugged and tweaked at the kite string, his eyes focused on *Shaheen* as it soared to join the others.

The orange and blue kite circled above them, tissue rippling on the wind, begging for more line. Jamie held the spool loosely, letting the kite gobble up the line, flying ever higher under Ali's watchful eye.

"*Pecha!*" came the cry from somewhere in the neighbourhood as a yellow kite zigzagged towards them – their first fight!

Ali bit his lip in concentration. The jousting began. The two kites swooped and rose back up, each trying to get the upper hand. Jamie watched Ali closely, playing out the line and then reeling it in – always making sure they had room to manoeuvre.

The kites began to tangle.

All of a sudden, the yellow kite went slack, drifting away on the wind, line dangling uselessly. "*Bo kata!*" Ali cried out. First kite to them.

Jamie glanced over at the rooftop where Sohail and the others had been last night. There was no sign of them yet.

Ali launched *Shaheen* back into battle. There were plenty of other duels to be had. Jamie licked his lips, getting a taste for Basant. Ali let him take the lead for a short while, and Jamie could feel the kite straining at the end of the line. It didn't feel like bamboo and paper; it felt alive, like an animal on a leash.

They flew for hours, well into the middle of the day. Two, three times they saw other kites drift off into the distance, cut by Ali's skill. Finally, around lunchtime, they caught sight of Sohail.

"*Pecha!*" A loud cry rang out, as Sohail launched a huge red beast up into the air. Up and up the kite rose. Jamie could see Sohail letting out hand after hand of string, until the kite was nothing more than a red dot flickering in the haze.

"We must follow," Ali said to Jamie. "Let out nearly as much line as we have." Jamie let the spool spin in his hands, round and round like a wheel. *Shaheen* rose into the sky, following Sohail's kite, seeking it out.

"How can you see what you're doing?" Jamie asked. "I can barely even make out either of them."

"You must also feel," said Ali. "How the kite is pulling, the way the line jumps. I can't see so well, but I can feel."

The two specks in the distance danced coyly with each other, neither fighter willing to make the first move, neither willing to commit. Would it be Ali or Sohail? Closer and closer the kites circled, Sohail teasing by darting his kite towards theirs, then pulling away at the last minute.

It was Ali who blinked first. "Watch!" he hissed as he brought the kite down sharply, aiming it straight towards the ground and the line of the red kite. Sohail reeled his kite away. Then Ali let out the line, and Sohail too changed tack, following. Suddenly Ali pulled hard, and the kite turned back on itself. "Got him!" he gasped.

Jamie could just make out *Shaheen* caught in a tangle, line cutting against line.

Jamie held his breath and waited, half expecting the string to go slack and to see *Shaheen* vanish into the distance. He could hear the blood pounding in his ears. Then a bellowing cry cut through the haze, "*Bo kata!*"

But it wasn't Sohail. It was Ali, his eyes wild, his arms in the air. "*Bo kata!*" Ali shouted again, jumping up and down.

"Howzat!" shouted Jamie. They'd done it! They'd taken Sohail's kite.

They reeled in the line as fast as they could. "Keep your eye on that kite," Ali grinned at Jamie. "We must see if we can catch it."

Once their kite was safely back on the roof, the boys raced down the stairs into Jamie's house.

"We did it!" Jamie called out to his mum, who was in the kitchen.

"I thought you might have," she laughed.

The boys fled out onto the deserted street, desperate to get hold of the drifting, red kite, but it was clear they would never find it. The kite had been too high when it was cut. Their red prize was long gone by now. They stopped running and stood at the end of the street. "Never mind," Ali laughed. "Let someone else enjoy it," he said, waving at the sky.

They began walking back to the house, when suddenly a shout came from above them, "Ali!" It was Sohail, leaning over the balcony railing of his house. "Wait there!" he ordered.

The front gate to the house swung open and Sohail and his friends filed out onto the pavement.

"You cut my line," Sohail spat.

"That's right," said Jamie, with a sudden boldness he wasn't feeling inside.

Sohail glared at him, and then he smiled. "*Shabash!*" Sohail clapped his hands together. "It was a good fight. Well done!" He came up to Ali and Jamie and shook their hands.

"You were the first ever to beat me," he admitted, "but the day isn't finished yet." He winked at Ali and Jamie as he turned to go back inside. "See you boys later at the cricket pitch!"

Jamie broke into a smile. "We wouldn't miss it for the world."